LET'S FIND OUT! ANIMAL LIFE

WHAT IS ANIMAL BEHAVIOR?

MONIQUE VESCIA

Britannica®
Educational Publishing

IN ASSOCIATION WITH

ROSEN
EDUCATIONAL SERVICES

Published in 2016 by Britannica Educational Publishing (a trademark of Encyclopædia Britannica, Inc.) in association with The Rosen Publishing Group, Inc.
29 East 21st Street, New York, NY 10010

Distributed exclusively by Rosen Publishing.
To see additional Britannica Educational Publishing titles, go to rosenpublishing.com.

First Edition

<u>Britannica Educational Publishing</u>
J. E. Luebering: Director, Core Reference Group
Mary Rose McCudden: Editor, Britannica Student Encyclopedia

<u>Rosen Publishing</u>
Hope Lourie Killcoyne: Executive Editor
Nicholas Croce: Editor
Nelson Sá: Art Director
Brian Garvey: Designer
Cindy Reiman: Photography Manager
Karen Huang: Photo Researcher

Library of Congresss Cataloging-in-Publication Data

Vescia, Monique.
What is animal behavior?/Monique Vescia.
     pages cm. — (Let's find out! Animal life)
Includes bibliographical references and index.
ISBN 978-1-62275-991-0 (library bound) — ISBN 978-1-62275-992-7 (pbk.) —
ISBN 978-1-62275-994-1 (6-pack)
1. Animal behavior — Juvenile literature. I. Title.
QL751.5.V47 2014
591.5 — dc23
                                                                                                2014038176

Manufactured in the United States of America

CONTENTS

INSTINCT AND LIFE LESSONS

Humans have always been fascinated by how animals behave. In the past, people survived by closely observing animal behavior. Our ancestors had to defend themselves against wild creatures and capture them for food.

Today, most people see wild animals in zoos more often than in nature.

Humans and chimpanzees share many similar behaviors.

Animals of the same species share many of the same behaviors.

Scientists observe animals both in the wild and in laboratories.

Scientists study two kinds of behavior in animals, instinctive and learned. Instinctive behavior is something an animal is born knowing how to do. For example, from birth, baby spiders know how to build a web. Other behaviors must be learned. Cheetah cubs learn to hunt by watching their mother catch prey. Learned behaviors can change over time. In this way, a species adapts to changes in its environment.

A **species** is a certain type, or kind, of animal or plant.

HOW ANIMALS COMMUNICATE

Over time, our ancestors developed systems of spoken and written language. But we also show other people how we feel without using words. One look at your friend's face will tell you if she is sad or mad.

Other animals communicate with sounds as well as with body postures, changing skin colors, and even scents. A hive of honeybees signals an alarm by emitting a strong banana-like smell. Humpback whales communicate over great distances by singing

Body postures and facial expressions help humans understand one another.

Humpback whales can communicate with each other over thousands of miles.

THINK ABOUT IT
A happy dog wags its tail, but a cat will lash its tail to show anger. How else do animals use their tails to communicate?

complex "songs." Methods of communication are an important form of social behavior in animals. Group members may share information about where food can be found. One coyote may expose his belly to another to prove he is not a threat. Scientists still have much to learn about how many creatures communicate with one another.

WHAT'S FOR DINNER?

Plants make their own food. Animals must feed on other living things to survive. Those that eat other animals are called carnivores, or meat eaters. Foxes, hyenas, and other meat eaters have sharp teeth and claws. Many of the animals they prey on, or eat, are herbivores, or plant eaters. This large group includes horses, antelopes, and many insects. Herbivores have teeth made for chewing grasses and

A lioness is close on the heels of her warthog prey.

nibbling leaves. Animals that eat both plants and animals are called omnivores.

Animals have many different feeding behaviors. Some, such as hummingbirds, eat all the time; others eat only rarely. An adult alligator can survive for a year without a meal. Animals eat a lot before they hibernate. They need to store up fat in their bodies for the long sleep.

This hedgehog might eat insects, berries, snakes, or bird eggs before hibernating.

FIGHT OR FLIGHT

Many threats to animals exist in the wild. Some creatures are born knowing how to defend themselves. Others learn this behavior from other members of the group. Certain animals protect themselves and their young by fighting back with sharp claws or fangs.

COMPARE AND CONTRAST

One survival instinct is called the fight-or-flight response. An animal will defend itself or flee when threatened. Compare and contrast how different animals react to danger.

A young antelope tries to flee a predator cheetah cub.

10

Will the young bobcat back off before the baby skunk sprays?

Some, like rattlesnakes, use sound to scare away an enemy.

Many creatures rely on chemicals to keep predators away. When cornered, a skunk will spray stinky liquid from the glands under its tail. The black-and-white stripes on its fur signal a warning: Stay away!

Other animals remain hidden until danger has passed. Some escape from threats with speed and by intelligence. By "playing dead," certain creatures fool predators. They remain stiff and lifeless until the animal loses interest. The cuttlefish is a master of camouflage. It changes colors and patterns to blend in with its background.

REPRODUCTIVE BEHAVIORS

All animals can reproduce. Male and female animals mate and produce young. This behavior helps make sure that a species will survive. A few animals, such as the sandhill crane, pair up with one mate for life. Most animals have multiple partners. Male bees, called drones, die after mating with the honeybee queen. Clown fish are born male but can change into a female if necessary.

Sandhill cranes usually produce two eggs every breeding season.

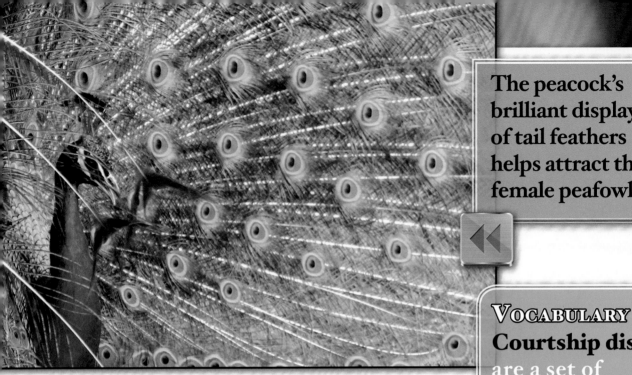

The peacock's brilliant display of tail feathers helps attract the female peafowl.

To human eyes, some animal courtship displays and mating behaviors can look very strange. Birds flash their colorful tails and perform crazy dances. Male ring-tailed lemurs release their scent at other males to shoo them away. A dance fly attracts its mate with a meal, wrapped up in silk like a present. The male frigate bird sends a "valentine." He inflates his red throat sac into what looks like a red, heart-shaped balloon.

How Animals Raise Their Babies

Animal babies enter the world in different ways. Some hatch from eggs. The eggs can be laid in the sand or kept safe in a parent's mouth. Some animals start out in one form and change to another during their lives. For example, frogs start out as swimming tadpoles. Others are born with the form they will have but need to finish developing. For example, rabbits have no fur and their eyes and ears are closed when they are born.

Animal parents have a variety of

behaviors, depending on the needs of their babies. Male emperor penguins incubate their eggs through Antarctic blizzards. In certain species, such as wolves, a pair of animal parents teaches their young how to survive. A newborn scorpion crawls onto its mother's back and stays there for up to 50 days. Other newborn creatures scurry away before their parents can eat them!

A pair of penguins keeps their egg warm in freezing weather.

Some mammals are born without fur, such as these newborn rabbits.

COMPARE AND CONTRAST

Think about the different ways animals take care of their young. Which animals are the most attentive parents? Which ones are the least attentive?

SOCIAL BEHAVIORS

By nature, human beings are social animals. We live in families, within larger communities. People need these social connections to survive. Many other animals live in social groups, too.

Mammal communities often have complex social structures. In gorilla groups, an older male, called a silverback, is in charge. Chimpanzees often cooperate to share child-rearing duties. The leaders

This baby chimp has a devoted and caring mother.

In an anthill, these social insects instinctively know how to work together.

of elephant families and orca pods are always female.

Smaller animals can band together to protect themselves from larger predators. In a group, a few animals may act as guards. They keep an eye out for danger while the others are eating or sleeping.

THINK ABOUT IT

The movements of fish swimming together in schools help confuse predators. How else do animals benefit from living in groups?

Social insects, such as ants, termites, and honeybees, work together in a colony or hive. Each insect has a specific job to do to keep the colony functioning.

LONE WOLVES

Many animals live in social groups. They depend upon other members of their own kind for survival. However, others are solitary by nature. Giant pandas usually avoid contact with other pandas. The solitary American badger leaves its den only at night to search for food. While lions live in groups called prides, tigers are solitary big

When disturbed, a badger will fight back by growling and biting.

cats. These endangered animals interact with other tigers only during mating season or when a mother tiger takes care of her cubs.

VOCABULARY
Solitary: growing or living alone.

Some species are social and solitary at different times. For instance, wolves may hunt in groups or alone. Solitary behavior has certain advantages. A lone wolf needs to find enough food for only one. Sickness spreads much faster in a group than from one solitary animal to another.

A wolf may howl to say "I'm here," or "Keep away!"

ON THE MOVE

Some species of animals migrate in large groups during the year. Because Earth's climate changes in different seasons, these animals keep on the move. Some fly, while others walk or swim. They travel to find fresh sources of water and food or to breed. Sea turtles and salmon migrate to lay

THINK ABOUT IT

Robins appear in gardens and parks during springtime. Are there other animals you notice arriving, or leaving, at certain times of the year?

Salmon use their sense of smell to find their way upstream.

Migrating monarch butterflies cluster on a tree to rest their wings.

their eggs in the same place year after year. Migration occurs throughout the animal kingdom.

Monarch butterflies fly for thousands of miles, from Canada far south to Mexico. Some whales give birth in warm waters and then head for colder waters rich with food. Other aquatic species swim up from the deep toward the warmer sea surface. Migrating animals may use visible landmarks like rivers or mountains to help them find their way. Some chart their positions by the Sun and the stars.

How Animals Sleep

All animals need rest to stay healthy. Some require very little sleep, while others need a lot. Giraffes sleep fewer than two hours each day. In contrast, brown bats are very sleepy creatures. Hanging upside down, this bat may snooze for 20 hours a day. Dolphins have a special ability. When they sleep, half of their brain stays awake. This allows them to breathe and keep alert for danger.

Hibernation is a very deep form of sleep. Animals hibernate to conserve energy and survive the cold winter when food may be scarce.

Bears in zoos sleep, but few hibernate like their wild cousins.

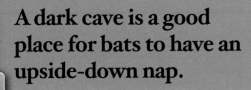

A dark cave is a good place for bats to have an upside-down nap.

COMPARE AND CONTRAST

How are the behaviors of animals that are active in the daytime different from those that are nocturnal?

Box turtles, hedgehogs, and dormice are just a few of the creatures that hibernate during the winter. A hibernating animal may appear dead. It barely breathes, and its body temperature drops very low.

Nocturnal animals, such as owls, wake up when others go to sleep. Owls have excellent night vision and silent wings. They hunt for other nocturnal animals.

Odd Couples

Animals usually prefer the company of their own kind. Sometimes, though, animals from different species team up. On the African plains, ostriches and zebras can often be found together. The zebra has a good sense of hearing and smell, but its eyesight is weak. Ostriches have excellent eyesight, but they don't hear very well. These two species of animals have learned to band together to help keep each other safe from danger. This is known as symbiosis.

Sometimes, both animals in a symbiotic pair benefit from each other's company.

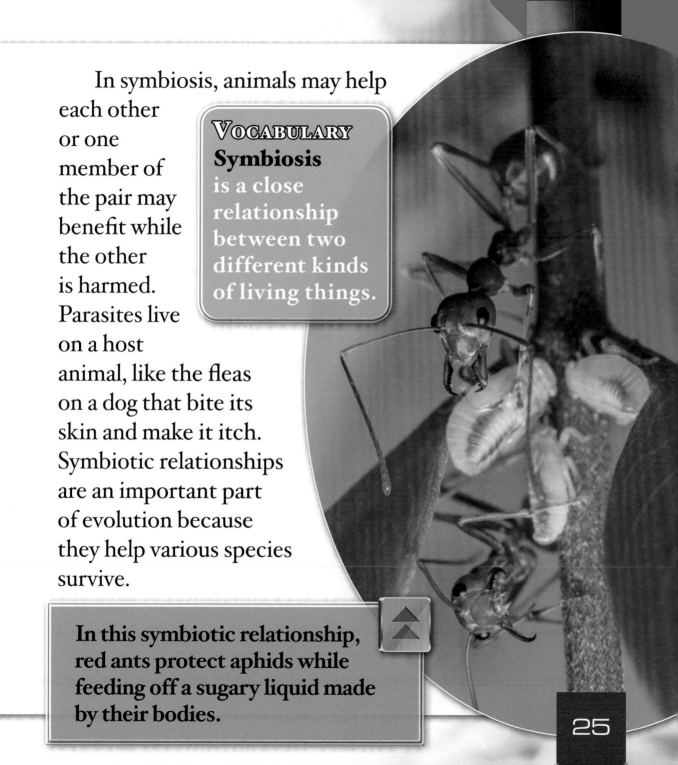

In symbiosis, animals may help each other or one member of the pair may benefit while the other is harmed. Parasites live on a host animal, like the fleas on a dog that bite its skin and make it itch. Symbiotic relationships are an important part of evolution because they help various species survive.

In this symbiotic relationship, red ants protect aphids while feeding off a sugary liquid made by their bodies.

HOW ANIMALS MOURN

Humans often feel very sad when a person they know dies. The dead body is treated with care and respect before it is buried in the ground or burned. People in different cultures hold special rituals to honor the dead.

Elephants seem to mourn the dead body of a family member.

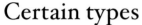

An orangutan mother gives her adult daughter a tender kiss.

Certain types of animals also seem to mourn their dead. An elephant will stroke the bones of a dead elephant with its trunk. Some bottlenose dolphin mothers refuse to leave their dead babies for many days. A healthy chimpanzee was observed to be so upset by the death of its mother that it stopped eating and eventually died.

Sometimes animals behave in ways that seem very human. However, we cannot assume that an animal acts for the same reasons that a person does. After much careful observation and study, scientists now believe that certain animals do experience grief.

THINK ABOUT IT

Human beings often cry when they lose a loved one. How might other animals express their grief?

SHARING EARTH

As civilizations developed, humans learned to domesticate animals that were once wild. They raised cattle for milk and meat, collected wool from sheep, and gathered eggs from chickens. These animals' behaviors changed over time as they became tamer. They learned to depend on people for food, water, and shelter. Today, humans also keep domestic animals as pets. They may treat their dog or pot-bellied pig like a member of the family.

New tools let us study wild animals in their natural habitats, or surroundings. The science of animal behavior has allowed us to better

Human and horse work together to keep these cattle moving.

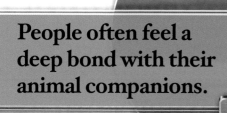

People often feel a deep bond with their animal companions.

understand animals and why they behave as they do. It may also provide clues about why we as human beings behave the way we do.

Human actions have brought about major changes in the many places where we live. Human behavior has important consequences for all the other animals with whom we share this planet.

GLOSSARY

adapt To change or adjust to a difference.

animal behavior Anything an animal does.

camouflage A way to hide or disguise something by covering it up or changing the way it looks.

carnivore An animal that eats other animals.

communication Exchange of information between individuals and groups.

cooperate To work or act together for a common benefit.

domesticate To adapt a plant or animal to make it useful to humans.

environment The climate, soil, and living things that support an organism.

evolution The process by which one living thing develops over time.

herbivore An animal that feeds on grass and other plants.

hibernation A very deep form of sleep, during which an animal's body temperature drops.

incubate To sit upon or warm eggs until they hatch.

instinctive Known automatically.

mammal A warm-blooded animal with hair on its body that nourishes its young with milk.

migration The movement of animals from one place to another during certain times of the year.

nocturnal Active at night.

parasite An organism that lives on and harms another organism.

predator An animal that lives by preying on others.

prey An animal hunted for food.

reproduction The process by which animals create offspring.

social Relating to the interactions between an individual and a group.

FOR MORE INFORMATION

Books

Hughes, Catherine D. *First Big Book of the Ocean.* Des Moines, IA: National Geographic Children's Books, 2013.

Jenkins, Steve. *The Animal Book: The Collection of the Fastest, Fiercest, Toughest, Cleverest, Shyest—and Most Surprising—Animals on Earth.* Boston, MA: HMH Books for Young Readers, 2013.

Marsh, Laura. *National Geographic Readers: Great Migrations: Amazing Animal Journeys.* Des Moines, IA: National Geographic Children's Books, 2011.

Page, Robin, and Steve Jenkins. *How to Clean a Hippopotamus: A Look at Unusual Animal Partnerships.* Boston, MA: HMH Books for Young Readers, 2013.

Spelman, Lucy. *National Geographic Animal Encyclopedia.* Des Moines, IA: National Geographic Children's Books, 2013.

Websites

Because of the changing nature of Internet links, Rosen Publishing has developed an online list of websites related to the subject of this book. This site is updated regularly. Please use this link to access the list:

http://www.rosenlinks.com/LFO/Behav

INDEX